A Gift of Faith

To:

From:

Date:

Marriage

A Fountain
of Grace

Written and Compiled by

Rosalie McPhee

Detail from *The Meeting* of Sts. Joachim and Anne,
painted by Marysia Kowalchyk

Design by Rob Huston
Artwork selected by Rosalie McPhee

First Printing, September 15th, 2001
Feast of Our Lady of Sorrows

Printed in Canada

MADONNA HOUSE PUBLICATIONS
COMBERMERE • ONTARIO • CANADA • K0J 1L0

www.madonnahouse.org

*To all couples called to
the vocation of marriage,*

*May you always rely on the
Fountain of Grace.*

Table of Contents

The bus was almost empty. Giving my ticket to the driver, I sat down and prepared for the two-hour ride home from college. This would give me time to think, to sort things out. For I was having difficulty breaking out of a painful relationship; one filled with duplicity and lies. My trust had been broken. Perhaps this time away with old friends and family would offer healing and a new perspective.

My thoughts were suddenly interrupted by the words: "Is anyone sitting here?" Looking up irritably, I saw a young man in a buckskin jacket. He was smiling expectantly, pointing to the seat beside me. He appeared familiar—perhaps from college. My abrupt glance around at the near-empty bus acknowledged my irritation and questioned whether this was just some bold come on. I really had no time for this! But his infectious grin, and polite request for permission made me drop my guard. I nodded my assent curtly. "No one here. Go ahead", I said closing my eyes and pretending to be asleep. Hopefully he would leave me alone.

He didn't—far from it. In no time, he drew me into conversation, and we began to talk openly about everything, and we were laughing together—real gut-aching laughter! How long had it been since I had experienced this heart-warming kind of merriment? Could I have guessed at this time that this was my soul mate, my beloved, the one to share my life and co-create our children with God and with me? During that two-hour ride, my whole life changed. It wasn't like falling "head-over-heels" in love. It was quiet, strong, sure—knowing somewhere deep down in my soul, before I knew in my mind—that this was the one whom I was created for, and who was created for me. It was confirmed somehow, when I learned that he was born on my first birthday! This was definitely the best present I ever received, even if I had to wait twenty years for him! It was the beginning of our journey together on the road of life—a road that would prove to be rocky and circuitous, but ever ascending upward to God.

The Little Mandate

Arise—go! Sell all you possess. Give it directly, personally to the poor.

Take up My cross (their cross) and follow Me, going to the poor, being poor, being one with them, one with Me.

Little—be always little! Be simple, poor, childlike.

Preach the gospel with your life—*without compromise!* Listen to the Spirit. He will lead you.

Do little things exceedingly well for love of Me.

Love... love... love, never counting the cost.

Go into the marketplace and stay with Me. Pray, fast. Pray always, fast.

Be hidden. Be a light to your neighbor's feet. Go without fears into the depth of men's hearts. I shall be with you.

Pray always. *I will be your rest.*

The Little Mandate was given to Catherine Doherty from the Holy Spirit as she listened intently to hear how God wanted her to live the Gospel. Many couples have heard the echo of these words in their hearts and have been blessed as they strive to live the Gospel wholeheartedly.

Introduction

Day after day Christian married couples are called to open their hearts ever more to the Holy Spirit, whose power never fails, and who enables them to love each other as Christ has loved us.

John Paul II, Homily, Sept. 11, 1987

Marriage is a road to holiness. The grace of the sacrament uplifts, strengthens, and leads us on our way to God. Although it is a magnificent, illuminated road, it is also narrow and rough, with countless jagged rocks, thorns and hurdles. Those are put there by a loving Father, not to trip us and make it impossible to continue, but rather to make us strong enough to withstand and ascend to the highest reaches where He dwells. He beckons, lavishes his grace, and even carries us along the most treacherous reaches. It is a road to walk hand in hand, sometimes skipping and cavorting joyfully, other times helping each other up when we fall, kissing each other's wounds, and comforting and encouraging one another through the darkest valleys. And yet, as we rise up out of each dark glade, we run and dance with lighter feet towards our goal—God's shining and glorious kingdom!

There are many times in marriage when we want to turn away, to refuse to grow and to be stretched. We think that by turning away, we can avoid the pain, but those are the very times that we need to take a deep breath, turn back to one another, and gaze into the soul of the one we were created for, and allow ourselves to be melted back into that oneness of our sacrament, and melted into God.

It came to us early on in our relationship that unless we kept drawing closer to one another, and learned to love more each day, we would gradually draw further apart, and a cold wind of indifference would seep into our sacrament. But in order to draw closer, we needed to be steadfast in submitting to the lessons that this path—this school of love—assigned us. In searching for guidance how to live marriage as a vocation, we found three rich sources: Scripture, the wisdom of our Church, and the spirituality of Catherine Doherty.

Our Holy Father sees the plan of our Father in heaven so clearly, and lovingly tries to impart it to us. He also sees the world around us, and all the forces that try to enslave and divide us in our marriages. But he continues to call us higher, and help us on our way, by pointing us to our God who made us, and by clearly reiterating the wisdom of our Holy Church.

Catherine's spirituality was essential to us on our path. In her first marriage, which was later annulled, she experienced real pain and heartbreak. In her second marriage, to Eddie Doherty, she at last found true love, rooted and centered in God. Her advice is down-to-earth, and yet she points us to the heights of a life together in God. The Little Mandate and the concept of *sobornost* apply so rightly to marriage, and this helped us to clarify our roles as husband and wife, and to continually climb towards the top of the mountain of God.

We cannot survive in marriage by being average, or by following the crowd. We need to be non-conformists, and follow what is written deep in our hearts. Sometimes we need to close our ears to the deafening sounds that tempt us or taunt us into believing that it is impossible to love faithfully for a lifetime. Let us turn our faces toward the light, and follow steadfastly the way that is illumined before us, one step at a time, always holding one another's hands, and being true helpmates as well as true lovers. Let us love with our whole beings, keeping nothing back; as we surrender to one another in love, learning the love we were created for, day by day.

To set out on the path of the married vocation means to learn married love day by day, year by year: love according to soul and body, love that "is patient, is kind, that does not insist on its own way... and does not rejoice at wrong."

John Paul II, *To the Youth of the World,*
on the Occasion of International Youth Year

The way of loving God is so very simple: the diapers, the baking, the laundry; sitting quietly, telling stories to the children, holding the hand of one's spouse. All are little acts of love, directed not only to one's family but also to God. This is what he wants...

    Listen to the dishes. Listen to the laundry. Listen to the work of the gardener or the farmer. A great and beautiful chorus is rising up from the hearts of men and women who believe.

    And the love of Jesus Christ responds to that chorus of love, because that is the way he worked for many years, writing us love letters.

Catherine Doherty, *Sobornost*

Sobornost
Unity in the Trinity

Holy Father, keep them in thy name, which thou hast given me, that they may be one, even as we are one.

John 17:11

So if there is any encouragement in Christ, any incentive of love, any participation in the Spirit, any affection and sympathy, complete my joy by being of the same mind, having the same love, being in full accord and of one mind.

Philippians 2:1–2

o you have any idea of the enormous power of your sacrament of marriage? You are a community, like the Trinity—father, mother, child—it is awesome—you should fall trembling on your knees before the wonder of your sacrament!"

She sat at the dining room table with us, speaking to us of marriage, exhorting us to live it to its full God-given potential. She took the salt and pepper shakers to represent Don and me, and grabbed the vitamin bottle to represent the child.

"You see—this is you, and your children, in this indivisible trinity of love—you have *everything* in each other! Your family is the image of the Trinity on earth!" She clasped the three bottles together tightly, to show the power of this invisible bond.

"This is *sobornost*—the unity between you which you receive from the Father and the Son and the Holy Spirit—you must learn to live it!"

Catherine Doherty was such a big presence. As soon as we met her, we knew that you listened to this lady. Our hunger for the truth brought us to her doorstep, like so many others, and she gave us the truth—the truth we needed to set us free. From then on, we sought to understand the mystery of this new word *sobornost*, a Russian word that can't really be translated into English adequately. From then on we would strive to understand it more and more and to "learn to live it". It became the focus and the ultimate goal in our marriage.

Sobornost is you and I being melted into God and having the same mind because it is totally plunged into him, melted into him.

Sobornost is a mystery, but it is a mystery of love. You don't penetrate love with your mind, with your head, because the head is absolutely useless for love... It is something so strange, so mysterious, so incredible that your head begins to spin when you think about it, meditate on it, contemplate it. It is like looking into a body of water, and suddenly seeing that water 'open up' in some kind of silvery depths... at the bottom of which is the face of Christ.

Catherine Doherty, *Sobornost*

When we discovered that Catherine had written a whole book on this strange concept of *sobornost*, we devoured it, always relating it to our marriage, and how it applied to our own sacrament. "You and I being melted into God and having the same mind…" How beautiful, how inspirational this was. Yes, our hearts sang as we continued to seek to understand.

Sobornost is something that one's heart catches from another heart. It is a mystery of union between, not only person and person, peoples and peoples, but between God and people. It is a sort of fire, for God has sent his Fire, the Holy Spirit, as an Advocate. He has done this so that—in total faith, trust, and love—we might turn to one another and blend with each other in the heart of Christ. We do this, not by holding hands, but by holding hearts.

Catherine Doherty, Sobornost

Holding hearts—this was a beautiful image— which showed us more and more that we had to find unity in our hearts, and in the heart of God, and to trust less in our minds to find agreement on things. Not that we were supposed to abandon all logic and rationality, but we were first to turn to one another and, through prayer, to blend together in the heart of Christ. Once we were able to both let go of our own ways, our preferences and opinions, then we could begin to hear *God's* way in each situation.

Sobornost is a strange manner of living. Sobornost is love in action. If you really love, you serve each other. It means that you never think of yourself; or rather you put yourself in the third place. God comes first; your neighbor is second; then yourself.

Catherine Doherty, Sobornost

Ah, now we were getting to something that jarred a little—this wasn't so comfortable! We had to *serve* each other, and put the other first. Coming from the "me" generation, of "doing our own thing", this didn't really appeal to us. Yet there was an insistent nudge…yes, this was true, too! It met a deep hunger and knowledge in us that this was what would bring us unity in our marriage.

Let us face the fact that, unless we live the Gospel — not only preach it, but live it — there can be no unity among us, no sobornost, no gathering of like minds. But few can agree on the Gospel. In order to live *the*

Gospel, one has to move through the life of Jesus Christ. That means abandonment, being rejected, being crucified.

There is no sobornost without crucifixion; it is through pain that one acquires a deep knowledge not found in books or by education. This deep knowledge, given by God and by God alone, builds the foundation of unity. And it is in those depths that one finds the foundation of sobornost, of unity.

Sobornost is never superficial. It is never temporary. It is always there like cool water offered from the cup of one's heart to all of one's brethren.

People united in sobornost are transparent.

Yes, there is much more to be said about sobornost! God has given us in sobornost a strange unity that could really shake the Church. Sobornost is the manifestation of that unity which Christ asked us to live and reflect, when he prayed to the Father that we "may all be one; even as thou, Father, art in me, and I in thee." (John 17:21)

Catherine Doherty, Sobornost

Oh dear, if we found it disturbing to have to put each other first and to serve one another, how about rejection, abandonment, crucifixion? Were we ready for this? Yet, even as this first fearful reaction came, it was followed again by that little song in our hearts...*This is My truth*.

And without this truth, we would flounder, and fail to live the fullness of our sacrament, or to experience the oneness God intended for us. We knew this was the way God was pointing out for us and for all married people, and we took the road of deepening *sobornost*.

Most Holy Trinity, we offer ourselves to you: body, soul and spirit. Allow us to share in the unity you know, and teach us how to always seek and follow that oneness in our sacrament. Give us the grace to be selfless and transparent, putting you first, and always seeking the good of the other before ourselves.

Listen to the Spirit. He will lead you.

The Little Mandate

Vocation of Marriage
Called by God Himself

Then the Lord God said, "It is not good that the man should be alone; I will make him a helper fit for him."

So the Lord God caused a deep sleep to fall upon the man, and while he slept took one of his ribs and closed up its place with flesh; and the rib which the Lord God had taken from the man he made into a woman and brought her to the man.

Genesis 2:18, 21–22

Jesus Changes
Water into Wine

Oneness of vocation, of love, of mind, heart, soul, and body—a man and woman bound by the soft, unbreakable bonds of an awesome sacrament—form a home.

Catherine Doherty, Dear Parents

Those "soft, unbreakable bonds" are a beautiful representation of the bonds of marriage. They make me think of a padded velvet cord—soft, beautiful, non-threatening, loving. There is a tendency to think of bonds in a negative sense, such as in bondage. Don and I were called to leave behind our old life and to become this new creation, where the two of us, though still two individual souls, became *one*. It means I could no longer think of what's best for me, but what is best for *us*. The bonds restrict us in a sense, in terms of fidelity to one another, and always considering the good of the other, but they are soft, gentle bonds that do not chafe unless we fight them. We don't lose anything by leaving behind the old; together we are more than the sum of our parts, becoming stronger as we surrender to this new oneness.

Mankind, to resemble God, must be a couple, two persons moving one towards the other, two persons whom perfect love will gather into unity. This movement and this love make them resemble God, who is Love itself, the absolute Unity of the three persons.

John Paul II, Homily, May 3, 1980

What an amazing statement, that "mankind, to resemble God, must be a couple"! It gives us another glimpse at that unfathomable mystery of two becoming one, and how we complement each other's masculine and feminine natures, to make us complete. It is God himself who gathers us into unity as we respond to him in our movement towards one another in love.

The vocation to marriage is written in the very nature of man and woman as they came from the hand of the Creator.

Catechism of the Catholic Church, 1603

Marriage is a vocation, a call of God to two people to become one, found a home, beget, bear, and raise children; and, in this glorious and very hard voca-

tion, to become saints themselves, and do all that is in their power to make saints of their children.

Catherine Doherty, Dear Parents

I hadn't thought of marriage as being a vocation until the time of my entry into the Catholic Church, when we had been married for seven years. It was an astounding discovery to realize that God had called each of us, from all eternity, to be together as one. How reassuring it was to know that, and to know that He would supply all we would need to fulfill our vows, no matter what difficulties we might encounter. What a comfort to know that he chose the very best person for me, to help get me to heaven, as well as each of our children, with all their virtues and faults. In His great economy he makes saints of us as we strive to make saints of our children.

Slowly, we begin to understand that the Catholic faith is not only a matter of attending Mass on Sundays and doing the bare minimum our Church requires, for even these practices of Catholicism are but means to an end. Living the Catholic faith is a way of life that embraces every minute of our wak-

ing and sleeping hours and permeates our lives at work, at home, in school, on a date, from the cradle to the grave.

Once we understand this, a change will take place in our hearts, and the ultimate goal of life will stand out more and more clearly. We shall know, and understand well, that we have been created to love. *We shall understand that all vocations we may embrace, including marriage, are* vocations to love.

Catherine Doherty, *Dear Parents*

Unless our faith became a way of life, we realized that we would not be able to survive for long. It was not a call to tacitly accept God and his teachings through his Church—we were called to *embrace* them. What a difference! It's something like the difference between a formal handshake and a big bear hug that knocks you off your feet!

The gift of the sacrament is at the same time a vocation and commandment for the Christian spouses, that they may remain faithful to each other forever, beyond every trial and difficulty, in generous obedience to the holy will of the Lord: "What therefore

God has joined together, let not man put asunder."
Familiaris Consortio, 20

Children of the sixties, searching for God, we were surrounded by people who had rejected many of society's norms and institutions, including marriage. When we announced to our friends our plans to get married, we met with open opposition. We ourselves really had no idea what this step would mean in our lives; we only knew we loved each other, and wanted a family.

At the time, marriage was a decision for us, a commitment, but I didn't really believe it would make a big difference in our lives. We believed in God, but were still searching for him in all directions except that of the Church. We had our love—what else did we need? God saw, and looked down lovingly at our ignorance and naïveté. As would so often be the case in our life together, he got us in the right place through our wrong (or at least faulty) reasons.

Calm and almost casual as we entered into the ceremony, it was as we were saying our vows that something happened to me—something overpowering, that caused my knees to suddenly shake. All at once I knew in my deepest heart that something huge, something amazing, something so much bigger than any of us was happening. Never having learned to kneel in my religious upbringing, I had the overpowering urge to do so now, at the realization that a hidden miracle was taking place: the two of us, created from different parents, in different parts of the world, were truly becoming *one*.

Lord, you created us and called us to this holy sacrament of marriage. Help us to leave behind the "me-first" attitude, and to surrender joyfully to those soft, unbreakable bonds. Give us the grace to always remember that marriage was your idea, and to rely on you for everything we need to live our vocation.

Arise—go! Sell all you possess.

The Little Mandate

One in Body
God's Gift of Sexual Love

I am my beloveds,
*   and his desire is for me.*
Come, my beloved,
*   let us go forth into the fields,*
*   and lodge in the villages;*
let us go out early to the vineyards,
*   and see whether the vines have budded,*
whether the grape blossoms have opened
*   and the pomegranates are in bloom.*
There I will give you my love.

Song of Songs 7:10–12

How softly our advents come to us...They herald their coming with a kiss. They speak louder, through the tender embrace of a man's arms. They sing their Te Deums, "We praise you, O God, ..." in a voice of thunder at the ecstasy of love, for it takes three to bring to us mortals our advents—a man, a woman, and God! At the last echoes of our Te Deum, the peace that surpasses all understanding comes to dwell with us, for where love is, God is, and there his peace dwells. Peace, stillness, and Mary's lullaby bring us sleep that gives us strength for the thousand tasks of tomorrow, and prepares us for the infinite graces to come.

Catherine Doherty, Dear Parents

Catherine speaks so eloquently of the ecstasy of love, when shared with and rooted in God. When we give our sexuality to God, and live according to his plan and his graces, we continue to grow closer to each other and to Him who made us. It is an ongoing progression in holiness, scaling the heights of union on the physical, spiritual, emotional and mental plane. From these heights, which seem sometimes like touching heaven, we settle into a peace that surpasses human understanding—a peace on all these levels of our being. And this peace and this unity and this sharing in Divine Love do indeed prepare us for whatever God has in store for us, and eventually for eternity.

Eat, O friends, and drink:
  drink deeply, O lovers!
I slept, but my heart was awake.
Hark! My beloved is knocking.
"Open to me, my sister, my love,
  my dove, my perfect one;
for my head is wet with dew,
my locks with the drops of the night."
I had put off my garment,
how could I put it on?
I had bathed my feet,
how could I soil them?
My beloved put his hand to the latch,
and my heart was thrilled within me.
I arose to open to my beloved,
and my hands dripped with myrrh,
my fingers with liquid myrrh,
upon the handles of the bolt.

Song of Solomon 5:1–5

In the Song of Songs the "language of the body" becomes a part of the single process of the mutual attraction of the man and woman, which is expressed in the frequent refrains that speak of the search that is full of nostalgia, of affectionate solicitude (cf. Sg 2:7) and of the spouses' mutual rediscovery (cf. Sg 5:2). This brings them joy and calm and seems to lead them to a continual search. One has the impression that in meeting each other, in reaching each other, in experiencing one's nearness, they ceaselessly continue to tend toward something: they yield to the call of something that dominates the content of the moment and surpasses the limits of the eros, limits that are reread in the words of the mutual "language of the body" (cf. Sg 1:7-8; 2:17).

John Paul II, General Audience, June 6, 1984

I think of Sts. Joachim and Anne as patron saints of marriage, and especially as mentors in teaching us to be holy in our lovemaking. God chose them to conceive a human being who was completely unblemished and perfect, and this suggests to me that they loved each other with a passionate but completely pure love.

Lord, you created our bodies to love one another in this magnificent way. Help us always to remember this, and to enjoy the fullness of love together, giving ourselves totally and joyfully to one another. Sts. Joachim and Anne, teach us to love passionately, with our bodies, souls and spirits!

Pray always. *I will be your rest.*

The Little Mandate

Purity in Marriage
Love, Lust, and Self-discipline

Thou madest Adam and gavest
*   him Eve his wife*
*   as a helper and support.*
From them the race of mankind
*   has sprung.*
Thou didst say, 'It is not good that
*   the man should be alone;*
*   let us make a helper for him like*
*   himself.'*
*   And now, O Lord, I am not taking this sister of*
mine because of lust, but with sincerity. Grant that I
may find mercy and may
grow old together with
her." And she said with
him, "Amen."

*   Tobit 8:6–8*

There is a special chastity for married folks. It consists in fidelity to their marriage vows, in faithfulness to one another, in modesty that remembers that each belongs to the other until death, and that neither can in speech, act, dress, or any other way, have any dealings with members of the opposite sex that, even in their shadowy connotations, savor of an imperfection against this shining, glorious virtue.

It would take a book to define in detail the fragile, fragrant and exquisite virtue of marital chastity to our lustful, forgetful world that worships the body beautiful as a god unto itself.

Catherine Doherty, Dear Parents

Because promiscuity is so prevalent in today's society, being "sexy" is a well-established norm in personal appearance, dress, and attitude. There are many people who are looking for a casual sexual partner, and so their purpose in their dress is to emphasize their sexuality to attract others for that purpose. Although God created our sexual nature, and it is beautiful, it can be (and often is) used for sinful purposes.

Catherine reminds us that it's not as simple as refraining from committing adultery, but even the "shadowy connotations" can break down a marriage.

Take flirting, for example. Many couples are very casual about their flirtations with others outside their marriage. They even do it in front of one another, sometimes purposely to make their spouse jealous. It becomes a habit, but is a language, a message being conveyed, and can cause sin and disruption.

Although within marriage we are called to give our bodies totally to the other, and to live the fullness of our sexuality wholeheartedly, this powerful gift is reserved for marriage alone. For this reason, we need to learn custody of our eyes and our minds, as well as our bodies. We must learn that, apart from our spouse, all others are simply our brothers and sisters in Christ, to be loved chastely without hint of anything sexual.

Lust is disordered desire for or inordinate enjoyment of sexual pleasure. Sexual pleasure is morally disordered when sought for itself, isolated from its procreative and unitive purposes.

Catechism Of The Catholic Church, 2351

It was after about three years of marriage that I began to sense something that bothered me in our sexual relationship. It wasn't there all the time, but the difference became apparent between the times of true communion, and times when we were merely objects to satisfy one another. This 'lust' began to be abhorrent to me.

When I finally tried to share this with Don, he didn't take it too well *at all*, at first. This was partly because it was so hard to put into words what I was feeling. It wasn't that I didn't like sex, or that he wasn't satisfying me. It was just that I noticed that the two experiences were so different, and one was so much better than the other. There was really no comparison. Somehow I only wanted the communion of our bodies, souls, and minds. The lustful embrace was only our bodies, and left a feeling of dissatisfaction and disappointment.

Having discovered this, I wondered if we might even be called to a life of celibacy. Fortunately, my spiritual director listened attentively and told me that God would tell Don too, if that was his call for us. After checking with Don, I realized that Don was most certainly *not* getting that message! Humbled, I turned back to Don and to finding holiness through our sexual relationship.

When I first began to sense lust I didn't really know what I was talking about; it was a deep and subconscious discovery, which it took many years to see more clearly, and to learn from. Fortunately, Don saw the truth that I was reaching for, and it became a journey we embarked on together. In seeking chaste sexual union, our relationship developed and was strengthened, and our sexual encounters grew in purity and at the same time intensity. This was rather a surprise, because people often mistake sexual purity for prudishness. It came to us as a great epiphany when we were finally able to see that we were to let God into our lovemaking, and allow Him to lead us. At first it was too much to envision God watching us as we made love. But then it seemed obvious that if we found it hard to imagine God looking at us making love, then we were still bound by a false shame in our nakedness before God, and in our appreciation of God's gift of sex in marriage.

The man said,
"This at last is bone of my bones
and flesh of my flesh;
she shall be called Woman,

because she was taken out of Man."

Therefore a man leaves his father and his mother and cleaves to his wife, and they become one flesh. And the man and his wife were both naked, and were not ashamed.

Genesis 2:23–25

Striving to grow in purity and closeness to one another in our sexual relationship, we also learned the important and inseparable connection between the pleasure of the unity we felt and our openness to life. It didn't mean that we had to be *trying* to conceive a child with every experience of conjugal communion, but that we wouldn't do anything to *prevent* conception. Following the natural rhythms of my body, and being aware when we *could* conceive, made the connection between the unitive and procreative aspects quite apparent. It was an ongoing process of discernment whether God was calling us to try and conceive another child, with the only exception being when I was pregnant. This meant we had to remain prayerfully open to God and his inspirations, and at the same time to look at the obvious practical aspects that might or might not make conception favorable at that time. The abstinence required in following these natural rhythms, although difficult at times, only strengthened our relationship, and helped us to grow in the virtues of self-control, patience, and concern for one another. And these in turn purified our sexuality in the process.

This discipline which is proper to the purity of married couples, far from harming conjugal love, rather confers on it a higher human value. It demands continual effort yet, thanks to its beneficent influence, husband and wife fully develop their personalities, being enriched with spiritual values. Such discipline bestows upon family life fruits of tranquility and peace, and facilitates the solution of other problems; it favors attention for one's partner, helps both parties to drive out selfishness, the enemy of true love; and deepens their sense of responsibility.

Humanae Vitae, 21

This covers a lot of ground! Aren't these all qualities that we can use in life and in our marriage in particular? They don't come naturally, but are learned through such "exercises" that Natural Family Planning assigns us. We come into the world as totally self-centered little beings, with our survival instincts fooling us into thinking that we are the center of the universe. Even in adolescence, this attitude is still fairly prevalent. Although reason tells us that others exist in the universe, we still tend to think of ourselves first. Life experiences, as well as the graces God imparts, can teach us and make us more selfless, but many couples enter marriage with the "me first" attitude, and are looking for a partner to fulfill their own needs. Sometimes it is hard to give in, to learn to put our spouse first. Children are the greatest teachers of this.

If a young person enters into the holy vocation of matrimony "to be loved," and both partners have the same idea, then who is going to do the loving?

Catherine Doherty, Gospel Without Compromise

Man is precisely a person because he is master of himself and has self-control. Indeed, insofar as he is master of himself he can "give himself" to the other.

John Paul II, General Audience, August 22, 1984

Lord, purify our hearts and minds and souls. Help us to turn away from all that is not holy, and reclaim the innocence that belongs to us in our bodily communion. Be with us as we love; inspire us and guide us to ever greater heights of unity and tenderness.

Pray, fast. Pray always, fast.

The Little Mandate

Co-Creators
with the Father
Procreative Love

God created man in his own image, in the image of God he created him; male and female he created them. And God blessed them, and God said to them, "Be fruitful and multiply".

Genesis 1:27–28

Married life is truly the school of sanctity where, with the birth of each child, Christ is born.

All Catholics are called to say Mary's "yes", but especially the husband and wife. They have the additional grace not only to give birth to Christ in their souls but also to beget other Christs in the children of their flesh and love.

Catherine Doherty, Dear Parents

God had faith in man; he entrusted the sources of life to him; he called man and woman to collaborate in his creative work.

John Paul II, Homily, March 5, 1983

I always wanted children. There seemed to be so little time between when my dolls were my 'babies' and the joy of giving birth to my first child. Don didn't have that same innate desire in the beginning, but he saw how great was *my* yearning for a child, and yielded trustingly, though somewhat hesitantly at first. But when he first held his own child in his arms, he was absolutely awed by the wonder and beauty of our child, and the privilege of participating in this miracle of life. From then, he was hooked, and welcomed and cherished each child as it was conceived and born, and he was grateful that he had responded to my initial longing for a child. Having a child who was "flesh of our flesh" brought the miracle of life so very directly into our lives. How amazing to see hints of each of us reflected in this new, tiny life!

The marriage union itself cannot be consumed in a selfishness for two: the love that unites the spouses seeks to extend itself in the child and to become the love of parents for their child, as proven by the experience of so many couples in past centuries and in our times as well: couples who have found in the fruit of their love the way to strengthen and orient themselves and, in certain cases, to recover and be renewed.

John Paul II, General Audience, July 20, 1994

The revealing sign of authentic married love is openness to life.

Truth and Meaning of Human Sexuality, 15

For our love to be really authentic, we must open our hearts to God and to life. Whether or not we are able to conceive, we are called to open willingness in co-operating with God as co-creators with Him. Our Holy Father exhorts us: "Do not be afraid of the children that may come; they are the most precious gift from marriage!" (Homily, May 7, 1988) This openness to life doesn't necessarily mean having a large family, or having as many babies as are biologically possible. It is more a state of mind, and an awareness that is meant to remain always during childbearing years—Is God asking us to bring another child into this world? Of course, when the question is asked over and over again as conditions change, we need to remember to listen for the answer. And since we are one in our sacrament, it needs to be an ongoing discussion in our lives together. It really enhanced and enriched our relationship to always have this continual discernment. It became the backbone of our communication; one approached with love, directness, and sometimes humor. It required great honesty and courage to look deep within at our state of mind, heart and soul, as well as the more obvious physical challenges before us. We couldn't fool ourselves, or each other, that everything was fine when we felt stretched to the limit and ready to break. It was important for each of us to know that about the other and to respond in tenderness and love, in many concrete ways, as we learned to live in "responsible parenthood".

Having young children, we get used to coping with the duty of each present moment. It takes a practiced act of will to sit back and reflect on how I'm doing. How am I *really* doing? Don and I learned that the oft-heard phrase "How are you doing?" did not require the usually accepted answer: "Fine". Rarely are we really fine, and with good friends, and especially our spouse, it should become a code phrase meaning "How are you deep inside—how is your heart, your soul, your mind? What is God saying to you? You can let down your natural coping defenses, and share your truth with me."

Fecundity is a gift, an end of marriage, for conjugal love naturally tends to be fruitful. A child does not come from outside as something added on to the mutual love of the spouses, but springs from the very heart of that mutual giving, as its fruit and fulfillment.

Catechism of the Catholic Church, 2366

Life is a gift, and the presence of the children make us ever more aware that whatever is beautiful and positive in life comes freely from God.

John Paul II, Homily, Jan 19, 1988

I was dreading having to tell my sister-in-law that we were expecting our sixth child. It wasn't that she didn't approve of our big family. In fact, it was the opposite—she envied us. She and her husband had been married for two years, and were trying desperately to conceive a child. She loved our children, and loved us, but I knew that our news, juxtaposed with her own infertility, could make her very sad. It reminded me of the Old Testament women: Hannah, Sarah and Elizabeth, who considered their barrenness a sign of God's disfavor.

What didn't help matters was that we were scheduled to have dinner together for the first time in months. How could we disguise our joy at the knowledge of this new little child in our midst? We had already waited three months to tell them.

Meeting at the restaurant, we exchanged hugs and greetings. It was so good to see them again! But our secret was still in the forefront of my mind. Sitting down, we started to look over the menu. Barb looked solemn, but there was still that beautiful twinkle in her eye. She could handle this: she was a strong woman. She loved us both.

But before we got a chance to say anything, she ran from the room in haste. We looked at her husband with concern, but he remained undisturbed, reading over the menu. When she returned, she looked a little peaked, but with shining eyes, she burst out:

"Oh, it's so wonderful... I feel so *sick*... I'm *pregnant*! And you'll never guess what... we're expecting TWINS!"

Our hearts leapt for joy at this news! How generous God is in his ways! That meal was a great celebration of the *three* new lives in our midst!

It must not be forgotten however that, even when procreation is not possible, conjugal life does not for this reason lose its value. Physical sterility in fact can be for spouses the occasion for other important services to the life of the human person, for example, adoption, various forms of educational work, and assistance to other families and to poor or handicapped children.

Familiaris Consortio,14

Infertility is a cross that only some couples are called to bear, but as the Holy Father points out, it can be a call to "other important services to the love of the human person". There is a very great need in many areas, and yet God has a plan for each individual couple. It is important for those that struggle with infertility to know that "even when procreation is not possible, conjugal life does not for this reason lose its value." Their love-making retains its uniting force because they themselves have not severed the two meanings of their conjugal communion—the procreative and the unitive aspects are still intact. They leave it in God's able hands, and are given the reward of unity of body, soul, and spirit.

Since God is the author of life, and created sexuality himself, it is a great privilege that He gives us a part in the decision to try and conceive new life. Our Church clearly teaches this, and is very sensitive to all the factors that might come into play in our discernment.

There are those who argue that Natural Family Planning is really no different from birth control. This is far from the truth, and this is clarified in Humanae Vitae: "in the former, the married couple make legitimate use of a natural disposition; in the latter, they impede the development of natural processes." Some people have the mistaken idea that they may have exceptional reasons that make use of Natural Family Planning impossible, such as extreme health risks, especially life-threatening ones. Our Mother Church is compassionate but clear on this point:

If, then, there are serious motives to space out births, which derive from the physical or psychological conditions of husband and wife, or from external conditions, the Church teaches that it is then licit to take into account the natural rhythms immanent in the generative functions, for the use of marriage in the infecund periods only, and in this way to regulate birth without offending the moral principles which have been recalled earlier.

Humanae Vitae, 16

Holding my belly, I stroked it gently. I wanted to communicate my love to this new little person that God had sent us. I tried to imagine the tiny body, about one inch long by now. I could picture the newly formed little hands and feet, and the minute beating heart.

We were on our way for a short vacation, before our busy summer retreats began, taking our six children to the Martyrs' Shrine in Midland, Ontario, and then staying with a priest friend in his rectory. After spending a wonderful day at the shrine, and marveling at the deepening understanding of the lives of these courageous martyrs, we headed to the rectory. I started to feel a strange sensation, and when we arrived, discovered that I was bleeding. A foreboding started to creep into me as Don and I drove to the hospital, leaving the others with Father Wilf.

Waiting for the doctor's word after the tests and wanting to hear: "Your baby's OK", I wasn't ready for his words when he entered.

"You have six children already? Oh well, you won't be having *this* one."

This left me stunned, empty, like I had been slapped in the face. Don held me and enclosed me with my shaking sobs in his strong, loving arms as the doctor made a quick retreat. Don's own tears mingled with mine, and it felt as if we were alone against the world. But we were together. We had each other, and we *did* have six beautiful children. Suddenly it seemed clear, like a veil had been lifted, what an amazing miracle each strong little life was. But the realization that I would never hold that little one in my arms created such an ache and an emptiness in me. My grief was strong, and long, more than I ever could have imagined. Would it ever go away?

A couple of weeks later, as a special grace one day, while praying and grieving for this child, a picture appeared in my mind very vividly. Our Blessed Mother, radiant and smiling, held a tiny baby in her arms, and looked with incredible love on him. I knew this was our child, and had now become her own. I was humbled, knowing that she was the mother I could only strive to be, and she could give him more than I ever could. He would never suffer, never be sick, never be sad. A new peace descended on me, and I knew that we had a little saint in heaven who would always take care of us, and whom I would meet some day.

I have set before you life and death, blessing and curse; therefore choose life, that you and your descendants may live, loving the Lord your God, obeying his voice, and cleaving to him.

Deuteronomy 30:19–20

Lord, what an awesome privilege you have given us, sharing with u s this miracle of new life. Not only do you give us children to love and raise for your Kingdom, but you give us the joy of sharing in the creation of these new souls with you. Help us always to be open to new life, and to allow you to be Lord of our lives.

Little—be always little! Be simple, poor, childlike.

The Little Mandate

Gift of Forgiveness
Healing the Wounds of Sin

Put on then, as God's chosen ones, holy and beloved, compassion, kindness, lowliness, meekness, and patience, forbearing one another and, if one has a complaint against another, forgiving each other; as the Lord has forgiven you, so you also must forgive. And above all these put on love, which binds everything together in perfect harmony.

Colossians 3:12–14

With God, every moment is the moment of beginning again.

Catherine Doherty, Kiss of Christ

There was an unspoken agreement between us that there was no "out" in our relationship, which allowed us to weather the storms that come in marriage. From the beginning, we resisted making threats: "I'll leave you if you…" or "I'll leave you if you don't…" Of course I know that there are some who suffer extreme cases—abuse that no human being should endure, but in the daily ups and downs and arguments and struggles, we must know that we will work it out somehow. The graces are there in our sacrament, if we remain open to them. When we pledge fidelity to one another, we pledge it forever, and our relationship rests on that rock-like foundation.

Let us truly join hands in deep forgiveness of one another. Let us reconcile ourselves to anyone with whom we are not yet reconciled. Let us forget any attachment to anything that isn't God. Let us enlarge the circle of love in our heart, so that it can encompass humanity, the humanity that flows around, through and by us. Such love is the love of God. Mercy flows from it. Forgiveness is part of it. Humility sings a song to it.

Catherine Doherty, *Kiss of Christ*

I was so angry with him, I could have spit! Talk about seeing red! He was just absolutely and maddeningly impossible! He just didn't understand about me; he cared more about other people than about me, or about his children. I ran outside, slamming the door—I had to get perspective, calm down, do something to regain my equilibrium. Running blindly, stumblingly towards the chapel, I nearly fell through the door. The silence and peace almost assaulted me, juxtaposed with my furious and frenzied feelings. I couldn't think or see anything clearly, everything was just swirling around in chaotic confusion.

Looking around, my eyes lit on the statue of Our Lady. She looked so calm and strong, with a look of love in that little smile on her face. Although this was a statue that my eyes looked upon, somehow deep inside I knew her real presence was with me, loving me, comforting me, understanding my deepest heart. I knew that she *knew*—everything—and that she, although quiet and humble and unassuming, had great power to help me. Glancing at the serpent pinned beneath her feet, I knew he was the one who was clouding my mind. He was the one who was trying to divide me from my spouse, the other half of the oneness we became when we said our vows.

My lips began the familiar prayer of consecration to Jesus through Mary, the only words I could find to pray: "…I give you my body and soul, my goods both interior and exterior… to follow after you all the days of my life, and to be more faithful to you than I have ever been before…" (See the back of the book for the full text of the prayer.)

What did it mean to be more faithful than ever before? It meant, quite obviously, that each day of my life, I had to try and be just a little bit more faithful than the day before. It wasn't necessary to do it all at once, or to expect to be that person that Jesus is calling me to be right away. But it was a call to keep trying, to keep growing, and not to give up. The Evil One wanted that, and pointed out and whispered in my ear all those annoying things about Don, stretching and inflating the truth, seemingly showing sympathy for me. And at the same time he was whispering in

Don's ear, as if he were really on his side. So who were we listening to, anyway? Not to each other.

A peace descended on me. It was palpable, awe-inspiring, and humbling. Whether Don was right or wrong didn't matter anymore; I had been wrong, and I needed to repair that wrong.

This new realization was so exciting that I came running back, and burst into the house, eager to share with Don all that had happened. But somehow the words I chose were wrong, and he felt accused. We couldn't seem to communicate, and the anger and upset came tumbling back. How could this be happening?! Panic started to set in again, but then something became clear to me. I was trying to use my inadequate intellect to describe a very deep and simple thing.

I reached out and took his hands, looked into his eyes, and said: "I'm so sorry, Don... I love you." Tears started to flow from his eyes, and mine, and we kissed each other with tender, salty kisses. We looked into each other's eyes, holding hands tightly, and prayed for protection for our sacrament. We prayed that we would always turn away from those beguiling whispers, and never let the sun set on our anger.

Be angry but do not sin; do not let the sun go down on your anger, and give no opportunity to the devil...be kind to one another, tenderhearted, forgiving one another, as God in Christ forgave you.

Ephesians 4:26–27; 32

Lord, we hurt one another, and hurt ourselves so often, that forgiveness must be a part of every day in our marriage. Give us the humility to ask forgiveness and to give forgiveness readily. Help us to let go of our opinions, and of always having to be right. Forgive us, Lord. Help us to start again, loving with your Love.

Love... love... love, never counting the cost.

The Little Mandate

Standing Under the Fountain of Grace

Allowing God In

For this reason I bow my knees before the Father, from whom every family in heaven and on earth is named, that according to the riches of his glory he may grant you to be strengthened with might through his Spirit in the inner man, and that Christ may dwell in your hearts through faith; that you, being rooted and grounded in love, may have power to comprehend with all the saints what is the breadth and length and height and depth, and to know the love of Christ which surpasses knowledge, that you may be filled with all the fulness of God.

Ephesians 3:14–19

The Sacrament of Marriage is a fountain of grace which, together with the grace of your Baptism and Confirmation, and the strength which comes from the Eucharist, will enable you, day by day, to accept sacrifices for each other's sake, to remain faithful in the face of every difficulty, trial and temptation, and in all ways to fulfill the demands of your calling as Christian married people!

John Paul II, Homily, Sept. 4, 1990

Our Holy Father isn't trying to tell us that marriage is easy, but he offers some guidelines for remaining faithful. Besides constant recourse to the Sacraments of the Eucharist and Confession, we have those lasting graces from our Baptism and Confirmation, which we sometimes forget about, but are there for our use. We need to "keep our pipes clean" in keeping right with God, and to not rely on our own strengths, or be discouraged by our own weakness. This image of a "fountain of grace" reminds us that the source is gushing, powerful, and limitless, if we will only stand under it.

*God, by his grace, gives us such great supernat-
ural help. Yes! Listen…listen to the wind…we are
not alone. Constantly with us, right by our side, is
the Dove. See! It's the Dove that is making the wind.
It's the wind of his gifts. With them, we can enter the
heart of another. With the gifts of love and tenderness and of the compassion of God, of Jesus Christ,
we can 'seal' the heart of another to ours, as ours is
sealed to God. That is the unity that must exist.*

*This unity transcends our emotions, our individ-
ualism, all things…because, you see, it is rooted in
God, whereas all other things are rooted in people,
in this world. But we can gather these things and lift
them up to God, as a finely wrought chalice.*

Catherine Doherty, Sobornost

The movement toward greater unity was our
shared purpose, and an ongoing growth in openness to God and his holy will. It meant continually reminding ourselves (and one another, in love)
that God is God and we are his creatures, and we
bend to kiss the ground that he created and
walked on when we kiss one another. This
required greater humility, and this doesn't usually
come all at once when we ask for it! It usually
means accepting humiliation, admitting we are

wrong, repenting over and over again for our rebellion against God, being misunderstood—but loving in the face of it all. It means deciding to love, asking for God's love, giving love that goes beyond feelings when we don't "feel like" loving.

Seeing Christ in each other, they will have to love each other with a great love. It will be a love of service and sacrifice, given joyfully, instantly, at all times, hard and easy. This will demand humility, the fertile soil of their souls, which must be cultivated constantly in order to grow the tremendous virtues of faith, hope, and charity. For without them, their marriage will wither before it has time to bring forth its first bud.

Catherine Doherty, Dear Parents

It wasn't something that we made a decision to do; we just kind of fell into it naturally, because we enjoyed each other's company so much, and it eventually became a habit. But it made such a difference to our marriage.

After breakfast it was our custom to go into the living room together and sit with our coffee or tea. A simple thing; but it was so much more than that. It was an inner attitude more than any-thing—a prayer, a stillness, a recollection, a focus, a listening and a sharing—about what God was doing in our lives at that particular time. There was such a constancy in it, but such an ebb and flow as we traversed the highs and the lows that marked all that came to us on that journey. We reflected on the day before, and anticipated what this day might hold, or the days ahead. Of course, the topic often revolved around our eight chil-dren, and how each was doing—physically, men-tally, emotionally, and spiritually.

We talked about our hopes and dreams for the future, and what God was teaching us at that time. Looking closely at our relationship, we assessed whether we were getting closer or more distant—it seemed it was one or the other. Depending on our life situation at that time, we would exhort, advise, comfort, encourage, admonish and inspire one another. These times rarely turned into fights or arguments or power struggles, because they were based on openness of our hearts and on being vulnerable and honest. It was a process of learning and growth, as we developed more trust and knowledge of one another's deepest selves.

Sometimes it was mundane, ordinary things we talked about. Other times it was breathtakingly profound. We processed the happenings of our lives together, and lifted them up to our loving Father, through tragedy and crisis as well as the mountaintops we shared. But all those times brought us just a little closer day by day, and allowed us to live that oneness more completely than the day before.

Lord, why do we always forget the source of our strength, and turn from the gushing font of grace that you provide for us every day in our sacrament. Help us to turn to you in all things, and stop relying on our own power and resources. We love you, Lord, and we put all our hope and trust in you.

Go without fears into the depth of men's hearts.

The Little Mandate

The Flowering Cross
A Sacrificial Love

Through him we have obtained access to this grace in which we stand, and we rejoice in our hope of sharing the glory of God. More than that, we rejoice in our sufferings, knowing that suffering produces endurance, and endurance produces character, and character produces hope, and hope does not disappoint us, because God's love has been poured into our hearts through the Holy Spirit which has been given to us.

Romans 5:2–5

"I promise to be true to you in good times and in bad, in sickness and in health. I will love you and honor you all the days of my life."

Rite of Marriage

How important those words are, spoken when we usually have no idea what those bad times will be, or what difficulties we will face. Even Jesus stumbled under the weight of his cross, and a cross isn't meant to be light and easy, or it isn't really a cross. They aren't usually ones we choose ourselves, and so we are required to surrender to whatever God sends us, knowing he has tailor made it for us.

The crucifix is such an important image to have before us, in every room if possible. It reminds us that there is nothing God asks of us which amounts to what he went through himself for us, and that there is nothing he asks us that we cannot do, with his help.

In order to live the Gospel, one has to move through the life of Jesus Christ. That means abandonment, being rejected, being crucified…. It is through pain that one acquires the deep knowledge that is not

*found in books or by education. This deep knowl-
edge, given by God and by God alone, builds the
foundation of unity. People thus united are* transparent; *and it is in those depths that one finds the
foundation of sobornost, or unity.*

Catherine Doherty, Sobornost

Suffering really makes us aware of our helpless-
ness and our total dependence on God. It seems
to have an ability to purify us, and to get rid of the
dross. It seems that when we truly surrender, we
become transparent, dropping our masks and pre-
tenses, so that our true selves can shine through.

Fr. John Powell said that we have the option
in our attitude to the suffering that comes our
way. He said we can either become bitter, or better. We have the choice.

*There is no doubt that along the road of married and
family life difficulties will be met. There have
always been difficulties, but be sure that you will
never be without the help from heaven needed to
overcome them. Be faithful to Christ and you will be
happy! Be faithful to the teaching of the Church and
you will be united by a love that grows stronger and*

stronger! Fidelity has not gone out of fashion! You may be sure that it is the families that are truly Christian that will bring the smile back to our troubled world.

John Paul II, Homily, May 7, 1988

"I must tell you the truth—I would say you have two years to live, at the most. The only possibility to extend that would be a heart/lung transplant. Take some time to think about it."

It was the feast of Our Lady of Guadalupe. This day was always a special day of grace and of celebration in our family. Don had asked me to come with him to his doctor's appointment, and then we would return home to celebrate with tortillas, Mexican music, and a piñata.

The doctor's words echoed in my ears and pierced my heart. They were words from a movie, or from someone else's life. We walked out of the office, and I was only aware of the effort it took to just put one foot in front of the other.

Don seemed to have a strength that I could not find in myself. There was a calm and a peace about him, which seemed supernatural. He held me and comforted me, encircling me with his strong arms and overflowing love.

He bundled me into the car, and took me to a restaurant nearby. From there he called the children to say we wouldn't be home for dinner   and we sat and talked heart to heart. I wasn't ready to go home; I couldn't celebrate now.

"Posie, this is the first day of the rest of our lives, and from now on we have to really live each day as if it is our last together. Whatever the future holds, the present is here for us, and we will love and forgive each day, like we never have before. I know the grace is there for whatever God allows us to go through. Let us not waste time on regrets from the past, or fears of the future, but live in the present moment."

Somehow he passed some of his strength and peace to me. As we drove home, it occurred to me that it was no coincidence that this had happened on Our Lady's special feast day. She would walk with us on our Way of the Cross, and would help us get through the days to come.

Christ dwells with them, gives them the strength to take up their crosses and so follow him, to rise again after they have fallen, to forgive one another, to "bear one another's burdens", to "be subject to one another out of reverence for Christ" (Eph 5:21; Gal

6:2) and to love one another with supernatural, tender and fruitful love. In the joys of their love and family life he gives them here on earth a foretaste of the wedding feast of the Lamb.

Catechism Of The Catholic Church, 1642

Lord, help us to accept joyfully the crosses you choose for us. May we always keep before us the image of your death on the Cross, and draw our strength from it. You know best for us, and we trust that all things work together for our good. Thank you Lord, for loving us enough to die for us, and allowing us to unite our suffering with your own.

Take up My cross (their cross) and follow Me,
going to the poor, being poor, being one with them,
one with Me.

The Little Mandate

Pilgrims on a Journey
Learning married love day by day

That very day two of them were going to a village named Emmaus, about seven miles from Jerusalem, and talking with each other about all these things that had happened. While they were talking and discussing together, Jesus himself drew near and went with them.

Luke 24:13–15

Marriage is a road to personal holiness, to witness, and to evangelization in the world.

John Paul II, Homily, April 2, 1987

Don was my road to holiness, like it or not, just as I was his. If he was difficult at times, that difficulty was to make me holy. It meant following Jesus' example in learning how to deal with each struggle, going beyond myself, to forgive, to love, and to be purified. When we were like sandpaper to each other, the friction was smoothing away the imperfections in one another. I was called to love Don just as he was, not as I wished he *could* be. All I could change directly was myself, and leave the rest up to God and Don. I was called to continually move away from selfishness toward selflessness.

The union of their characters: to love a being is to love him such as he is, it is to love him to the extent of cultivating in oneself the antidote of his weaknesses or his faults, for example, calm and patience, if the other manifestly lacks them.

John Paul II, Homily, May 3, 1980

There is a resonance in me when I think of myself as the "antidote of his weaknesses". It sums up so well the lived-out reality of our call to marriage. In the mystery of how two people can really become one, it follows that we can try to make up for our spouse's weakness. But an antidote is really much more than making up for something. In the dictionary (American Heritage College Dictionary, Third Edition—Houghton Mifflin) it is defined as "a remedy or other agent used to neutralize or counteract the effects of a poison". This is an interesting image, because our sins *are* like poison—to others and to ourselves, and to our unity. From our deep love and unconditional acceptance of one another, we can indeed defuse the negative effects of each other's transgressions. We still have to take responsibility for our own sins of course, and stand before God alone when we die, but we can truly help one another to progress along the road to holiness.

Just as the Christian life requires continual conversion; so married life requires the couple to make constant and generous efforts to deepen their communion.

John Paul II, Homily August 17, 1985

Can you imagine the depths of unity that must exist between a husband and wife who mutually seek to find God through one another rather than in one another.

God wants their relationship to be a totality of love for Him. And because He loves them so passionately—and because He wants to hand them Himself so totally—He keeps calling them to an ever-greater faith, to a higher plateau, to a closer union with Him.

Catherine, Doherty, Donkey Bells

I stared in surprised recognition at the simple note card - it had been almost 30 years since I had seen it last. Of course Mom would have saved it; she saved everything, even bits of string tied together and rolled into balls, or carefully ironed wrapping paper. For once I was really thankful for this pack-rat quality in her. It was our wedding invitation. Avoiding anything extravagant or showy, I had designed a linocut for the card, which was hand-written.

In the ensuing years, I had forgotten about the symbol I had chosen. It was an acorn, and inside the acorn, a full-grown oak tree. It symbolized our hope for the future—that great things would come from that acorn we were planting.

My mind went back to that young, idealistic, and naïve couple we were. How little we knew of life and of marriage, and yet we thought we were so wise! We had no idea how much we had to learn from one another, and to teach one another, and to learn from the children we would co-create with God. Life was full of possibilities and dreams, and it seemed like we had forever to live them.

As we said the words "I promise to be true to you in good times and in bad, in sickness and in health", we couldn't really imagine any bad times or serious sickness. We seemed invulnerable in our optimism and zeal for life. When we promised: " I will love you and honor you all the days of my life", we couldn't imagine either of our lives ending.

On looking back on our twenty-six years of marriage, I am grateful for every moment we shared. I am glad we had that idealism, that thirst for life and truth and goodness, and I am glad that we were innocently ignorant of all that would follow.

Really, it was *all* good, even the most difficult things, because we *shared* them, and learned and grew on our spiritual journey together. From the beginning, we saw our life as a school of love, and knew that it was all a preparation for the eternal life to come. We would often laugh together, and say "Do you think we're out of kindergarten yet?!" It was just one of our silly little jokes.

I keep being reminded of the image of whether you see the glass half-full or half-empty. They are both true, but it's an attitude, a way of seeing. With a 'glass-half-empty attitude', one could say that our oak tree got cut down when it was only half grown with Don's death in 1997. Or one might say that it got struck by lightning, and the half that was him died. But in the 'glass-half-full attitude', which I know is God's attitude, I know that the tree is very much still alive and growing, in our children, our grandchildren, and those yet to be born, on an on. Our love was the seed, and it couldn't have happened without that. Sometimes, when we have a family gathering, I like to draw back into the shadows, and watch these sweet people who have come from our love, with all their life and vitality—as they play and love and laugh and cry together. Life goes on without me doing anything, and the tree continues to grow and stretch its roots into the deep soil of faith. I know that our lives on earth are only blinks in the eternity we have to look forward to, when nothing can separate us ever again.

Truly, truly, I say to you, unless a grain of wheat falls into the earth and dies, it remains alone; but if it dies, it bears much fruit. He who loves his life loses it, and he who hates his life in this world will keep it for eternal life. If any one serves me, he must follow me; and where I am, there shall my servant be also; if any one serves me, the Father will honor him.

John 12:24–26

Lord, we know we are pilgrims on this earth, and that our true home is in heaven with you. Help us to remember this always, and to travel this road with faith and perseverance, holding one another's hands in love and simplicity. Light our path, and guide us along the way. Give us peace and courage to face whatever we may encounter, our eyes always fixed on the glorious goal at the end of our journey.

Preach the Gospel with your life—
without compromise!

The Little Mandate

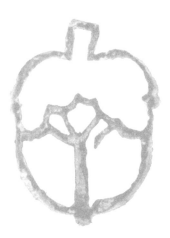

This acorn and full grown oak tree inside symbolized our hope for the future on earth and in eternity.

The tree remains very much alive in our children, their children, and the generations to come, for all eternity.

Love endures! Love reigns!

Act of Consecration
to Jesus Through Mary

(St. Louis de Montfort's Consecration)

I, _____, a faithless sinner—renew and ratify today in your hands, O Immaculate Mother, the vows of my Baptism; I renounce forever Satan, his pomps and works; and I give myself entirely to Jesus Christ, the Incarnate Wisdom, to carry my cross after Him all the days of my life, and to be more faithful to Him than I have ever been before.

In the presence of all the heavenly court I choose you this day for my Mother and Queen. I deliver and consecrate to you, as your slave, my body and soul, my goods, both interior and exterior, and even the value of all my good actions, past, present and future; leaving to you the entire and full right of disposing of me, and all that belongs to me, without exception, according to your good pleasure, for the greater glory of God, in time and in eternity.

Amen.

Notes

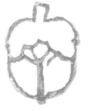

Notes

Notes

Acknowledgements

We would like to express our gratitude to the following for permission to use quotations:

Harmony Media, Inc., Gervais, OR, for permission to quote from The Teachings of Pope John Paul II on CD-ROM and The Illustrated Catholic Bible on CD-ROM.

Scripture quotations are taken from:

The Revised Standard Version Bible, Catholic Edition, copyright 1965 and 1966 by the Division of Christian Education of the National Council of the Churches of Christ in the USA. Used by permission. All rights reserved.

MADONNA HOUSE PUBLICATIONS
COMBERMERE • ONTARIO • CANADA • K0J 1L0

The aim of our publications is to share the Gospel of Jesus Christ with all people from all walks of life.

It is to awaken and deepen in our readers an experience of God's love in the most simple and ordinary facets of everyday life.

It is to make known to our readers how to live the tender, saving life of God in everything they do and for everyone they meet.

Madonna House Publications is a non-profit apostolate of Madonna House within the Catholic Church. Donations allow us to send books to people who cannot afford them but most need them all around the world.

Thank you for your participation in this apostolate!

How to Contact Us

Telephone:	1-613-756-3728
Fax:	1-613-756-0103
Address:	Madonna House Publications 2888 Dafoe Rd Combermere ON K0J 1L0
E-mail:	publications@madonnahouse.org
Web Site:	www.madonnahouse.org

Parents: Enter more deeply into your truest and most central vocation!

Mothering, lovingly written by Rosalie McPhee, explores the sanctuary of love that God intends the family to be, with the mother as its heart. She shares telling anecdotes from her storehouse of experiences as a mother and emphasizes that motherhood is a mission of service and love.

This book contains a call to mothers everywhere who are hungering for the truth that is their soul's sustenance, and searching for a clarity in the lived-out reality of their vocation.

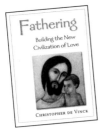

Fathering, by Christopher de Vinck (a father of three, and award-winning author of *The Power of the Powerless* and *Simple Wonders*), likewise discloses the majesty of fatherhood as a spiritual vocation. There is scriptural and traditional support for the father's role as protector and guardian of his family and a revelation of the glory of fatherhood as a path of sacrifice—a true imitation of Christ.

This book offers concrete help to fathers who wish to enter more deeply into their true vocation.

Mothering by Rosalie McPhee • 64 pages • ISBN 0-921440-60-X
Fathering by Christopher de Vinck • 64 pages • ISBN 0-921440-61-8
Each book: $6.95 ($8.95 Canadian)
Order Toll Free: 1-888-703-7110